GRUMPY CAT'S
KNITTING NIGHTMARES

More than 15 miserable projects for you & your friends

DOVER PUBLICATIONS, INC.
MINEOLA, NEW YORK

Grumpy's owner and model: Tabatha Bundesen
Photography: Tommy Muller
and

Grumpy Cat™

Grumpy Cat and Related Artwork © and ® Grumpy Cat Limited
www.GrumpyCats.com Used Under License

Copyright

Copyright © 2016 by Dover Publications, Inc.
All rights reserved.

Bibliographical Note

Grumpy Cat's Knitting Nightmares: More Than 15 Miserable Projects for You and Your Friends
is a new work, first published by Dover Publications, Inc., in 2016.

Library of Congress Cataloging-in-Publication Data

Names: Grumpy Cat, author. | Grumpy Cat Ltd.
Title: Grumpy Cat's knitting nightmares : more than 15 miserable projects for
  you and your friends.
Other titles: Knitting nightmares
Description: Mineola, New York : Dover Publications, Inc., [2016]
Identifiers: LCCN 2016015007| ISBN 9780486806112 | ISBN 0486806111
Subjects: LCSH: Knitting—Patterns. | Cats—Equipment and supplies. | Dress
  accessories.
Classification: LCC TT825 .G755 2016 | DDC 746.43/2—dc23 LC record available at
https://lccn.loc.gov/2016015007

Manufactured in the United States by LSC Communications
80611101   2016
www.doverpublications.com

CONTENTS

GRUMPY CAT'S
KNITTING NIGHTMARES

Welcome to
my world
. . . NOT!

FIERCE KITTY HAT
DESIGNED BY CAROL J. SULCOSKI

SKILL LEVEL

Easy

SIZES

Feline S (L) Sample is shown in size S.

Note: Small will fit up to 12in/30.5cm head circumference; Large will fit over 12in/30.5cm head circumference. Ribbing provides stretch for some flexibility in fit.

FINISHED MEASUREMENTS 4½ (5½)in/11 (14)cm high

MATERIALS

- Lion Brand® Lion's Pride® Woolspun® 3½oz/100g, 127yds/116m (80% acrylic, 20% wool)—one ball: #102 Aquamarine
- Two size US 10 (6mm) circular needles, 24in/61cm length OR SIZE TO OBTAIN GAUGE
- Size US 9 (5.5mm) circular needle, 24in/61cm length
- Cable needle
- Tapestry needle

GAUGE

10½ sts and 22 rnds = 4in/10cm in St st on larger needles. TAKE TIME TO CHECK GAUGE.

STITCH GUIDE

3/3C Slip next 3 stitches to cable needle and hold in front, knit next 3 stitches, knit 3 stitches from cable needle.

Note: The photo on page 5 shows the hat with the cable in the back.

HAT

With larger circular needles, **Needle 1** CO 16 (20) sts, **Needle 2** CO 20 (20) sts. Join to work in the rnd, being careful not to twist sts—36 (40) sts.

Rnds 1–3: Needle 1 [k2, p2] 4 (5) times, **Needle 2** [k2, p2] to end of rnd.

Rnds 4, 6–7: (Begin cable) **Needle 1** [k2, p2] 4 (5) times, **Needle 2** k2, p2, k6, p2, [k2, p2] 2 times.

Rnd 5: Needle 1 [k2, p2] 4 (5) times, **Needle 2** k2, p2, 3/3C, p2, [k2, p2] 2 times.

Rnds 8–21 (25): Rep last 4 rnds 3 (4) times, then work Rnds 4–5.

SHAPE CROWN

Rnd 22 (26): Needle 1 [k2, p2, k2, p2tog] 2 times, k0 (2), p0 (2), **Needle 2** k2, p2, k6, p2, k2, p2tog, k2, p2—33 (37) sts.

Rnd 23 (27): Needle 1 [k2 p2tog, k2, p1] 2 times, k0 (2), p0 (p2tog), **Needle 2** k2, p2tog, k6, p2tog, k2, p1, k2, p2tog—28 (31) sts.

Rnd 24 (28): Needle 1 [k2tog, p1] 4 (5) times, **Needle 2** k2tog, p1, k6, p1, k2tog, p1, k2tog, p1—21 (23) sts.

Rnd 25 (29): Needle 1 k2tog 4 (5) times, **Needle 2** k2tog 3 times, k1, k2tog 3 times—11 (12) sts.

Rnd 26 (30): Needle 1 k2tog 2 times, k0 (k1), **Needle 2** k2tog 3 times, k1—6 (7) sts.

Rnd 27 (31): Needle 1 k2tog (k3tog), **Needle 2** k2tog 2 times—3 sts.

Work I-cord on rem 3 sts until I-cord measures 4in/10cm. Cut yarn leaving a long tail. Thread tail through rem sts, gather tightly and fasten off. Weave in ends. Lightly steam block if desired, and tie I-cord into knot.

EARFLAPS

With smaller needle, pick up and knit 7 sts along one side edge of cap.

Rows 1–7: K—7 sts.

Row 8 (RS): Ssk, k to last 2 sts, k2tog—5 sts.

Row 9 (WS): K.

Rows 10–11: Rep Rows 8–9—3 sts.

Work I-cord on rem 3 sts until tie measures 9in/23cm. Cut yarn leaving a long tail, thread tail. Through rem sts, gather tightly and fasten off, weave in ends.

Rep on other side for second earflap.

WHY DO I HAVE TO LOOK SO ADORABLE?

NO-WAY COWL
DESIGNED BY SYLVIA BO BILVIA

SKILL LEVEL

Easy

SIZES

Feline S (L) Sample is shown in size S.

Note: Small will fit up to 12in/30.5cm head circumference; Large will fit over 12in/30.5cm head circumference. Ribbing provides stretch for some flexibility in fit.

FINISHED MEASUREMENTS 4in/10cm x 14in/35.5cm

MATERIALS

• Brooklyn Tweed Loft 1¾oz/50g, 275yds/251m (100% wool)—one skein: Fossil

• One pair size US 7 (4.5mm) needles OR SIZE TO OBTAIN GAUGE

• Two decorative buttons

GAUGE

40 sts and 20 rows = 4in/10cm in St st. TAKE TIME TO CHECK GAUGE.

COWL

CO 40 sts.

Row 1 (WS): [P2tog leaving the second st on the left needle] across to last stitch, p1.

Row 2 (RS): [K2tog through the back loop leaving the second st on the left hand needle] across to last stitch, k1.

Rep Rows 1–2 until work measures 14in/35.5cm.

Rep Row 1, BO.

FINISHING

Sew BO edge to the side near CO edge as in photo. Weave in ends. Sew on buttons for decoration.

GO AWAY SCARF
DESIGNED BY SYLVIA BO BILVIA

SKILL LEVEL
Easy

FINISHED MEASUREMENTS 5in/12.5cm x 30in/76m

MATERIALS

- Brooklyn Tweed Shelter 1.75oz/50g, 140yds/128m (100% wool)—one skein: Fossil
- One pair size US 5 (3.75mm) needles OR SIZE TO OBTAIN GAUGE
- Tapestry needle

GAUGE

18 sts and 27 rows = 4in/10cm in St st. TAKE TIME TO CHECK GAUGE.

SCARF

CO 23 sts.

Rows 1–5: K—23 sts.

Row 6 (WS): K3, p to last 3 sts, k3.

Row 7: K5, p2, k4, p1, k4, p2, k5.

Row 8: K3, p1, k2, p4, k3, p4, k2, p1, k3.

Row 9: K3, p2, k4, p2, k1, p2, k4, p2, k3.

Row 10: K3, p5, k2, p3, k2, p5, k3.

Row 11: K7, p2, k5, p2, k7.

Row 12: K3, p3, k2, p7, k2, p3, k3.

Rows 13–192: Rep row 7–12.

Rows 193–198: K, BO.

SCARF CHART

KEY

- ☐ Knit on RS and Purl on WS
- ⦿ Purl on RS and Knit on WS

Note: Odd number rows are RS, even number rows are WS.

FINISHING

Block scarf to finished measurements. Add fringe evenly along ends.

CAT COLLARS
DESIGNED BY VANESSA PUTT

SKILL LEVEL
Easy

FINISHED MEASUREMENTS 5½in/14cm long and ⅝in/1.5cm wide
(not including the cat collar)

MATERIALS

• Lion Brand® Bonbons® Beach Collection 8 x 35oz/10g, 28yd/26m (100% cotton)—one ball each: Turquoise (A), Yellow (B), Red (C), and White (D)

• One pair size US 2 (2.75mm) needles

• Cat collars ¼in/.6cm wide in desired size

• Tapestry needle

GAUGE

29 sts and 38 rows = 4in/10cm in St st. TAKE TIME TO CHECK GAUGE.

GRUMPY COLLAR

With A, CO 45 sts using a provisional CO.

Rows 1, 3 (RS): K1, p1, k to last 2 sts, p1, k1.

Rows 2, 4 (WS): K1, p1, k1, p to last 3 sts, k1, p1, k1.

Rows 5–9: Work in St st and seed st border as established. Using B, work letters from chart as desired.

Rows 10–13: Work even in St st with seed st border.

Place 45 CO sts on needle, use kitchener stitch to join ends of work into a tube. Weave in ends and slide over cat collar.

FEED ME COLLAR

Work as for Grumpy Collar using C for background and D for letters.

ALPHABET CHART

COLOR KEY

- ☐ MC
- ▧ CC

11

LOUSY CATNIP MOUSE
DESIGNED BY LORI STEINBERG

SKILL LEVEL
Easy

FINISHED MEASUREMENTS Diameter 3½in/9cm

MATERIALS

- Lion Brand® Bonbons® Nature Collection 8 x 35oz/10g, 28yd/26m (100% cotton)—one ball each: Tan (A), Dusty Rose (B), and Chocolate Brown (C)

- One set (5) double-pointed needles size US 4 (3.4mm) OR SIZE TO OBTAIN GAUGE

- Stitch marker

- Polyester stuffing

- Tapestry needle

- Catnip (optional)

GAUGE

24 sts and 35 rnds = 4in/10cm in St st. TAKE TIME TO CHECK GAUGE.

BODY (make 2)

With A, CO 8 sts. Divide evenly on 4 dpns. Join to work in the rnd, being careful not to twist sts, pm for beg of rnd.

Rnd 1: K.

Rnd 2 (inc): Kfb 8 times —16 sts.

Rnds 3–5: K.

Rnd 6 (inc): [M1, k1] around—32 sts.

Rnds 7–11: K.

Rnd 12 (inc): [M1, k1] around—64 sts.

Rnds 13–14: K, BO.

EARS (make 2)

With B, work Rnds 1–6 as for head—32 sts.

Knit 1 rnd, BO.

FINISHING

Block pieces, sew ears to one piece of body for front, using photo as guide for placement.

Face

With 2 strands of C held tog, make 2 French knots for eyes. With B, embroider nose and grumpy mouth, using photo as a guide. Cut 6 strands of C for whiskers and attach to each side of nose.

Tail

Cut 9 strands of C, 12in/30.5cm long. Tie tog with a knot and thread through center of back, keeping knot on WS. Braid, holding 3 strands tog. Tie a knot, and trim.

Sew body tog, leaving an opening for stuffing. Stuff lightly, add catnip (optional), and sew closed.

NO PLAYING CAT TOY
DESIGNED BY LORI STEINBERG

SKILL LEVEL  Easy

FINISHED MEASUREMENTS Diameter 3in/7.5cm

MATERIALS

• Lion Brand® Bonbons® Brights Collection 8 x 35oz /10g, 28yd/26m (cotton)—one ball: Red

• One set (5) double-pointed needles size US 4 (3.4mm) OR SIZE TO OBTAIN GAUGE

• Stitch marker

• Polyester stuffing

• Tapestry needle

GAUGE

24 sts and 35 rnds = 4in/10cm in St st. TAKE TIME TO CHECK GAUGE.

STITCH GUIDE

K1, P1 Rib: (odd number of sts).

Row 1 (RS): K1, [p1, k1] across.

Row 2 (WS): P1, [k1, p1] across.

Rep Rows 1 and 2 for k1, p1 rib.

I WON'T BE PLAYING ANYWAY.

14

CIRCLE

CO 45 sts. Divide evenly on 4 dpns. Join to work in the rnd, being careful not to twist sts, and place marker for beg of rnd.

Rnds 1–2: K—45 sts.

Rnd 3 (inc): [K5, M1]—54 sts.

Rnds 4–8: K.

Rnd 9 (dec): [K4, k2tog] around—45 sts.

Rnds 10–11: K, BO.

SLASH

CO 5 sts, work in k1, p1 rib for 1½in/4cm from beg, BO in rib.

FINISHING

Sew CO edge of circle to BO edge, stuffing lightly and evenly. Repeat with the slash and sew it diagonally to inside of circle, using photo as a guide.

DOGGIE VOODOO DOLL
DESIGNED BY LORI STEINBERG

SKILL LEVEL
Easy

FINISHED MEASUREMENTS 9in/23cm long x 3in/7.5cm wide

MATERIALS

- Lion Brand® Bonbons® Nature Collection 8 x 35oz/10g, 28yd/26m (cotton)—2 balls each: Cream (A), Dusty Rose (B), and Chocolate Brown (C)

- One set (5) double-pointed needles size US 4 (3.4mm) needles OR SIZE TO OBTAIN GAUGE

- Stitch marker

- Polyester stuffing

- Tapestry needle

GAUGE

24 sts and 35 rows = 4in/10cm over St st. TAKE TIME TO CHECK GAUGE.

BODY (make 2)

With A, CO 14 sts.

Row 1 (RS): K—14 sts.

Row 2: P.

Row 3 (inc): K1, M1, k to last st, M1, k1—16 sts.

Rows 4–7: Rep Rows 2–3—20 sts.

Work even in St st until piece measures 2½in/6cm from beg.

BO 2 sts at beg of next 6 rows. BO rem 8 sts.

HEAD (make 2)

With A, CO 8 sts.

Row 1 (RS): K—8 sts.

Row 2: P.

Rows 3 (inc): K1, M1, k to last st, M1, k1—10 sts.

Rows 4–7: Rep Rows 2–3 2 times—14 sts.

Rows 8–16: Work even in St st.

Row 17 (dec): K1, skp, k to last st, k2tog, k1—12 sts.

Row 18: P.

Rows 19–22: Rep Rows 17–18 2 times—8 sts.

BO rem 8 sts.

FRONT PAWS (make 2)

With A, CO 12 sts. Divide evenly on 4 dpns. Join to work in the rnd, being careful not to twist sts, and place marker for beg of rnd.

Work even in St st until piece measures 1½in/4cm from beg.

Next rnd (dec): [Skp, k2, k2tog] 2 times—8 sts.

Divide sts evenly on 2 needles and BO using 3-needle BO method.

HIND LEGS (make 2)

With A, CO 12 sts. Divide evenly on 4 dpns. Join, being careful not to twist sts, and place marker for beg of rnd.

Work even in St st until piece measures 2in/5cm from beg.

Next rnd (dec): [Skp, k2, k2tog] 2 times—8 sts.

Divide sts evenly on 2 needles and BO using 3-needle BO method.

EARS (make 2)

With C, CO 5 sts. Knit 1 row, purl 1 row.

Row 1 (RS): K—5 sts.

Row 2: P.

Row 3 (inc): Kfb, k to last 2 sts, kfb, k1—7 sts.

Rows 4–6, 8: Work even in St st.

Rows 7, 9 (dec): Skp, k to last 2 sts, k2tog—3 sts.

Rows 10–17: Work even in St st, BO.

NOW HERE'S A TOY I CAN STICK MY CLAWS INTO.

TAIL

With A, CO 10 sts. Work even in St st until piece measures 2in/5cm from beg, end with a WS row.

Next row (dec): [Skp, k1, k2tog] 2 times—6 sts.

Work 7 rows even in St st.

Next row (dec): K1, k2tog, skp, k1—4 sts.

Work 4 rows even in St st.

Next row (dec): Skp, k2tog—2 sts.

Next row: P2tog. Fasten off. Cut yarn leaving a long tail. Fold tail in half lengthwise and sew seam.

FINISHING

With B, embroider heart on front using duplicate stitch. With 2 strands of C held tog, embroider x's for eyes and straight stitch for snout, using photo as a guide. With C, embroider claws on paws, using photo as a guide. Sew body pieces tog, stuffing lightly. Sew head pieces tog, stuffing lightly. Stuff legs and sew to body. Sew on ears and tail. Wrap C around neck 5 times for collar.

BED HEAD CAT HAT
DESIGNED BY KATHARINE MALLER

SKILL LEVEL

Easy

SIZE
One size, to fit an adult woman

FINISHED MEASUREMENTS
Circumference 18in/45.5cm, Height 8in/20cm

MATERIALS
• Lion Brand® Lion's Pride® Woolspun® 3.5oz/100g, 127yds/116m (80% acrylic, 20% wool)—one ball each: #126 Coffee (A), #123 Taupe (B)

• One set (5) double-pointed needles size US 10½ (6.5mm) OR SIZE TO OBTAIN GAUGE

• Stitch marker

• Tapestry needle

GAUGE
13.5 sts and 18 rows = 4in/10cm in St st. TAKE TIME TO CHECK GAUGE.

STITCH GUIDE
K1, P1 Rib: (odd number of sts).

Row 1 (RS): K1, [p1, k1] across.

Row 2 (WS): P1, [k1, p1] across.

Rep Rows 1 and 2 for k1, p1 rib.

HAT

With A, CO 56 sts. Join to work in the rnd, being careful not to twist sts, and place marker for beg of rnd.

Rnds 1–9: K1, p1 rib.

Rnd 10: K.

Change to B. Work even in St st until hat measures 5in/12.5cm from CO edge.

CROWN SHAPING

Rnd 1: [K2tog, k6] 7 times—49sts.

Rnd 2 and all even Rnds: K.

Rnd 3: [K2tog, k5] 7 times—42sts.

Rnd 5: [K2tog, k4] 7 times—35sts.

Rnd 7: [K2tog, k3] 7 times—28sts.

Rnd 9: [K2tog, k2] 7 times—21sts.

Rnd 11: [K2tog, k1] 7 times—14 sts.

Rnd 13: K2tog 7 times—7 sts. Cut yarn leaving a long tail, thread tail through rem sts, gather tightly and fasten off.

EARS (make 2)

With A, CO 26 sts. Join to work in the rnd, being careful not to twist sts, and place marker for beg of rnd.

Rnd 1 and all odd Rnds: K.

Rnd 2: [K1, k2tog, k7, ssk, k1] 2 times—22sts.

Rnd 4: [K1, k2tog, k5, ssk, k1] 2 times—18sts.

Rnd 6: [K1, k2tog, k3, ssk, k1] 2 times—14sts.

Rnd 8: [K1, k2tog, k1, ssk, k1] 2 times—10sts.

Rnd 10: [K1, k3tog, k1] 2 times—6 sts.

Rnd 11: K. Cut yarn leaving a long tail, thread tail through rem sts, gather tightly and fasten off.

FINISHING

Position ears as desired and sew in place. Weave in ends.

GET OFF MY BED PILLOW COVER

DESIGNED BY CIRILIA ROSE

SKILL LEVEL
Easy

FINISHED MEASUREMENTS 13in/33cm square

MATERIALS

- Lion Brand® Lion's Pride® Woolspun® 3½oz/100g, 127yds/116m (80% acrylic/20% wool): 2 balls #098 Fisherman (A); 1 ball each: #126 Coffee (B), #102 Aquamarine (C), #123 Taupe (D)

- Black embroidery floss

- Size US 10½ (6.5mm) needles

- Tapestry needle

- Pillow 12in/30.5cm square

GAUGE

12 sts and 22 rows = 4in/10cm in St st. TAKE TIME TO CHECK GAUGE.

BACK

Row 1: With A, CO 37 sts, K1, [p1, k1] across.
Row 2: K the purl sts and p the knit sts.
Rep Row 2 for Seed st until piece measures about 7in/18cm from beg.

FRONT

Row 1 (RS): K.
Row 2: P.
Rows 3–4, 17–20: With B, rep rows 1–2.
Rows 5–29: Work color chart in St st for Face using the intarsia method.
Continue in Seed st until work measures approximately 29in/74cm from beg. BO in pattern, fasten off leaving tail for finishing.

FINISHING

Eyes

Embroider pupils in eyes with black embroidery floss. With B, embroider horizontal satin sts for eyelids. Fold pillow cover with ends overlapping 3in/7.5cm on back. Sew side seams. Weave in ends. Insert pillow.

PILLOW CHART

COLOR KEY

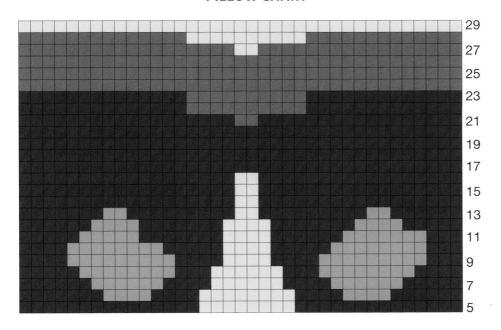

☐	Fisherman (A)
■	Coffee (B)
■	Aquamarine (C)
■	Taupe (D)

29
27
25
23
21
19
17
15
13
11
9
7
5

WISHY-WASHY WASHCLOTH
DESIGNED BY LISA MILLAN

SKILL LEVEL
Easy

FINISHED MEASUREMENTS 11¼ in/28.5cm x 9¼in/23.5cm

MATERIALS

• One 2oz/57g ball of any worsted weight 100% cotton yarn in any color

• One pair size US 7 (4.5mm) needles OR SIZE TO OBTAIN GAUGE

• Tapestry needle

GAUGE

15 sts and 22 rows = 4in/10cm in St st. TAKE TIME TO CHECK GAUGE.

WASHCLOTH

CO 43 sts.

Rows 1–4, 6, 8 (RS): K.
Rows 5, 7, 9: K4, p35, k4.
Row 10: K16, p1, k8, p1, k17.
Row 11: K4, p14, k1, p6, k1, p13, k4.
Row 12: K18, p6, k19.
Row 13: K4, p17, k1, p17, k4.
Row 14: K20, p1, k1, p1, k20.
Row 15: K4, p10, k3, p2, k1, p3, k1, p2, k2, p11, k4.
Row 16: K13, p4, k8, p6, k12.
Row 17: K4, p8, k7, p6, k6, p8, k4.
Row 18: K11, p8, k4, p9, k11.
Row 19: K4, p6, k4, p3, k3, p4, k2, p4, k2, p7, k4.
Row 20: K11, p2, k1, p2, k1, p2, k4, p3, k1, p1, k1, p4, k10.
Row 21: K4, p6, k4, p1, k1, p1, k4, p3, k2, p1, k2, p1, k2, p7, k4.
Row 22: K12, p7, k3, p10, k11.
Row 23: K4, p8, k9, p3, k6, p4, k1, p4, k4.
Row 24: K8, p1, k5, p6, k2, p8, k4, p2, k7.
Row 25: K4, p3, k3, p6, k5, p2, k5, p5, k2, p4, k4.
Row 26: K8, p2, k6, p4, k3, p2, k8, p3, k7.

Row 27: K4, p3, k4, p8, k1, p3, k3, p6, k3, p4, k4.

Row 28: K8, p3, k8, p1, k11, p5, k7.

Row 29: K4, p3, k8, p15, k2, p2, k2, p3, k4.

Row 30: K7, p2, k6, p2, k8, p5, k1, p5, k7.

Row 31: K4, p3, k5, p2, k4, p9, k2, p4, k3, p3, k4.

Row 32: K7, p3, k2, p3, k12, p2, k4, p3, k7.

Row 33: K4, p3, k3, p3, k1, p15, k3, p2, k2, p3, k4.

Row 34: K7, p2, k2, p2, k17, p1, k2, p3, k7.

Row 35: K4, p3, k1, p2, k2, p19, k2, p1, k2, p3, k4.

Row 36: K7, p4, k22, p1, k1, p1, k7.

Row 37: K4, p3, k2, p24, k3, p3, k4.

Row 38: K7, p2, k26, p1, k7.

Row 39: K4, p31, k1, p3, k4.

Rows 40, 42, 44: K.

Rows 41, 43, 45: K4, p35, k4.

Rows 46–50: K. Bind off. Weave in ends.

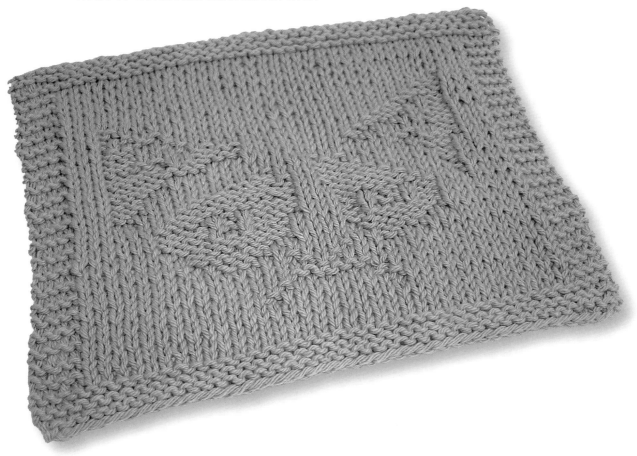

Note: Please see chart for Wishy-Washy Washcloth on page 59.

WHATEVER GADGET HOLDERS
TO FIT SMARTPHONE AND TABLET

DESIGNED BY CORINA COOK

SKILL LEVEL

◖■□□ **Easy**

FINISHED MEASUREMENTS

SMALL 6in/15cm x 3½in/9cm

LARGE 10in/25.5cm x 8in/20cm

MATERIALS

• Kraemer Yarns Perfection Worsted 3.5oz/100g, 200yds/183m (30% merino, 70% acrylic)—one ball each: Peep (A), Cliffs (B), Sand (C), April Shower (D), Coral Belle (E), and Onyx (F)

• One pair size US 8 (5mm) needles OR SIZE TO OBTAIN GAUGE

• Tapestry needle

GAUGE

18 sts and 20 rows = 4in/10cm in St st. TAKE TIME TO CHECK GAUGE.

SIDES (make 2)

With A, CO 27 (45) sts.

Row 1: K2 (4), p across—27 (45) sts.

Row 2: K across.

Rows 3–18: (40) Rep rows 1–2. BO.

Follow color chart to work duplicate stitches over the stockinette ground. Begin 2 rows down from the top in the 1st (3rd) K st. Embroider mouth.

CHART FOR TABLET

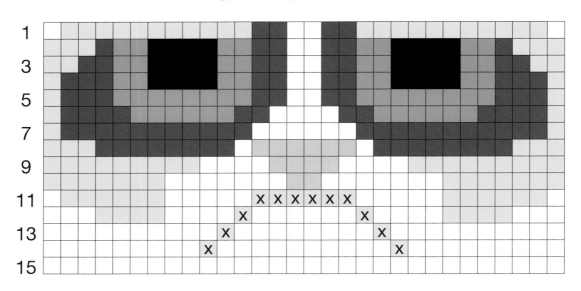

CHART FOR SMARTPHONE

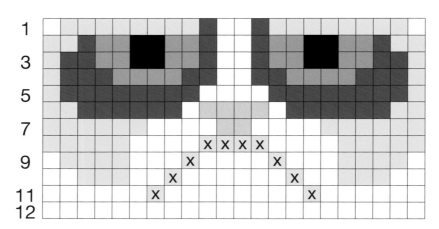

COLOR KEY

- ☐ Peep (A)
- ■ Cliffs (B)
- ■ April Shower (D)
- ☐ Coral Belle (E)
- ■ Onyx (F)
- ☒ Embroider

EARS (make 2)

Using two strands of B, CO 8 (10) sts, leaving a tail for sewing.

Rows 1, 3, 5: P.

Row 2: [K1, p1] across—8 (10) sts.

Row 4: K1, k2tog, k to last 3 sts, ssk, k1—6 (8) sts.

For Large only: Rep Rows 4–5—6 sts.

Row 6 (8): K1, k2tog, ssk, k1—4 sts.

Row 7 (9): P1, p2tog, p1—3 sts.

Row 8 (10): K1, ssk—2 sts.

Row 9 (11): P2tog, fasten off.

FINISHING

Sew 3 sides together leaving garter stitch edge open. Sew ears on top edge as pictured. Weave in ends.

DO THESE GADGETS HAVE A GRUMPY SETTING?

MONDAY MORNING COFFEE SLEEVE
DESIGNED BY KATHARINE MALLER

SKILL LEVEL
Easy

SIZE

One size—fits most 12–20oz/340–567g coffee cups

FINISHED MEASUREMENTS Circumference 9in/23cm, Height 4¼in/11cm

MATERIALS

• Lion Brand® Bonbons® Nature & Beach Collections 8 x 35oz/10g, 28yd/26m (100% cotton)—one ball each: Black (A), Red (B), White (C), Turquoise (D), Chocolate Brown (E), Cream (F), and Dusty Rose (G)

• One set (5) double-pointed needles size US 2 (3.0mm) OR SIZE TO OBTAIN GAUGE

• Tapestry needle

• Stitch marker

GAUGE

24 sts and 35 rows = 4in/10cm in St st. TAKE TIME TO CHECK GAUGE.

CUP COZY

With A, CO 54 sts. **Note:** Cozy is worked flat.

Rows 1–3: [K1, p1] across—54 sts.

Rows 4–32: Working in St st, follow Rows 1–28 of chart working 3 repeats across.

Rows 33–35: [K1, p1] across. BO in pattern.

FINISHING

With G, embroider frowns on cat faces as shown in the photograph. Seam sides of piece together to form cozy. Weave in ends.

CUP CHART

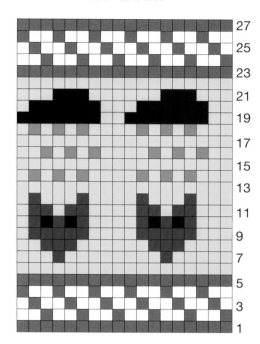

27
25
23
21
19
17
15
13
11
9
7
5
3
1

COLOR KEY

- ■ Red
- ■ Black
- □ White
- ■ Chocolate brown
- ■ Cream
- ■ Turquoise

I HATE MORNINGS . . . ESPECIALLY MONDAY MORNINGS.

MINI ME GRUMPY CAT PLUSH

DESIGNED BY KRISTIN EKSUZIAN

SKILL LEVEL

Intermediate

FINISHED MEASUREMENTS Height 8¼in/21cm

MATERIALS

- Lion Brand® Vanna's Choice® 3½oz/100g, 170yds/156m (100% acrylic)—one skein each: #099 Linen (A), #100 White (B), #125 Taupe (C), and #108 Dusty Blue (D)

- One pair size US 8 (5.0mm) straight needles OR SIZE TO OBTAIN GAUGE

- One set (5) double-pointed needles size US 8 (5.0mm)

- 2 stitch holders

- Stitch markers

- Tapestry needle

- Straight pins, embroidery needle

- Small amount of pink and black embroidery floss

GAUGE

17 sts and 24 rows = 4in/10cm in St st. TAKE TIME TO CHECK GAUGE.

STITCH GUIDE

Short Row Wrap and Turn (w&t)

On RS row, slip next stitch purlwise wyib. Bring yarn forward, then slip the stitch back onto left needle. Return yarn to back. One stitch is wrapped. Turn the work. Use the same method on WS row, bringing the yarn back and then forward.

HEAD

Wind 2 small balls of C and A and 1 of B for intarsia face detail at center.

With straight needles and A, CO 21 sts.

Row 1: K.

Rows 2, 4: P.

Row 3: K1, M1R, k5, M1R, k9, M1L, k5, M1L, k1—25 sts.

Row 5: K1A, M1RA, k7A, M1RA, k1A, k5B, w&t; p3B, w&t; k4B, w&t; p5B, w&t; k6B, K1A, M1LA, k7A, M1LA, k1A—29 sts.

Row 6: P11A, p7B, p11A.

Row 7: K10A, M1LA, k1C; k1B, M1LB, k5B, M1RB, k1B, k1C, M1RA, k10A —33 sts.

Row 8: P10A, M1RA, p2C, p9B, p2C, M1LA, p10A—35 sts.

Row 9: K10A, M1LA, k3C, k2B, k2togB, k1B, sskB, k2B, k3C, M1RA, k10A.

Row 10: P10A, M1RA, p4C, p1B, sspB, p1B, p2togB, p1B, p4C, M1LA, p10A.

Cut second ball of C, carry first ball on WS of B.

Row 11: K10A, M1LA, k5C, k2togB, k1B, sskB, k5C, M1RA, k10A.

I LIKED YOU BETTER AS A BALL OF YARN.

Rows 12, 14: P10A, p6C, p3B, p6C, p10A.

Row 13: K10A, k6C, k3B, k6C, k10A.

Row 15: K11A, k5C, k3B, k5C, k11A.

Row 16: P13A, p4C, p1B, p4C, p13A. Cut B.

Row 17: K15A, k5C, k15A.

Row 18: P16A, p3C, p16A. Cut C and second ball of A.

Row 19: With A, k.

Row 20: P1, [p2, p2tog] across to last 2 sts, p2—27 sts.

Row 21: K2 ,[k2tog, k1] across to last st, k1—19 sts.

Row 22: P1, p2tog across to last 2 sts, p2. Cut yarn, leaving a long tail. Thread tail through rem 11 sts, gather tightly and fasten off, weave in ends.

EARS (make 2)

With straight needles and C, CO 7 sts.

Rows 1, 3: K1, p5, k1.

Rows 2, 4: P1, k5, p1.

Row 5: K1, p2tog, p1, ssp, k1—5 sts.

Row 6: P1, k3, p1.

Row 7: K1, yfwd, sp2p, k1—3 sts.

Row 8: P1, k1, p1.

Row 9: Sk2p. Cut yarn, leaving a long tail. Thread tail through rem sts, gather tightly and fasten off, weave in ends.

BODY

With dpns and A, CO 21 sts. Join to work in the rnd, being careful not to twist sts.

Rnd 1: K.

Rnd 2: K3, [M1, k5] across to last 3 sts, M1, k3—25 sts.

Rnd 3: K4, pm, k17, pm, k4.

Rnd 4: K to marker, M1R, sl marker, k17, sl marker, M1L, k to end of rnd—27 sts.

Rnd 5: K.

Rnds 6–14: Rep rows 4–5 4 times, rep row 4—37 sts.

Rnd 15: K10, sl marker, transfer 7 sts to holder for right front leg, CO3, k3, CO3, transfer 7 sts to holder for left front leg, sl marker, k10—29 sts.

Rnd 16: K.

Rnd 17: K to marker, M1R, sl marker, k9, sl marker, M1L, k to end of rnd—31 sts.

Rnds 18–21: Rep rows 16–17 2 times—35 sts.

Rnds 22–31: K.

Rnd 32: [K3, k2tog] around—28 sts.

Rnd 33: [K2, k2tog] around—21 sts.

Rnd 34: [K1, k2tog] around—14 sts.

Rnd 35: K2tog around. Cut yarn, leaving a long tail. Thread tail through rem 7 sts, gather tightly and fasten off, weave in ends.

FRONT LEGS (make 2)

Rnd 1: With dpns and A, k 7 sts from holder, pick up and knit 1 st from left side of opening, pick up and knit 3 sts from BO edge, pick up and knit 1 st from right side of opening, join to work in the rnd—12 sts.

Rnds 2–3: K.

Rnds 4–12: Cut A. With C, k.

Rnds 13–17: Cut C. With B, k.

Rnd 18: [K2, k2tog] around. Cut yarn, leaving a long tail. Thread tail through rem 9 sts, gather tightly and fasten off, weave in ends.

BACK LEGS (make 1 right and 1 left)

With straight needles and A, CO 8 sts.

Rows 1–9 WS rows only: P.

Row 2: K1, M1R, k6, M1L, k1—10 sts.

Row 4: K1, M1R, k8, M1L, k1—12 sts.

Rows 6, 8: K.

Row 10 (Right leg only): K to last 3 sts, k2tog, k1—11 sts.

Row 10 (Left Leg only): K1, k2tog, k across—11 sts.

Row 11: P.

Rows 12–15: Rep rows 10–11 2 times—9 sts.

Row 16: K6, k2tog, k1, CO4. Switch to dpns and join to work in the rnd—12 sts.

Rnd 17: K.

Rnds 18–24: Cut A. With B, k.

Rnd 25: [K2, k2tog]. Cut yarn, leaving a long tail. Thread tail through rem 9 sts, gather tightly and fasten off, weave in ends.

TAIL

With C and dpns, CO 7 sts. Work I-cord until work measures 2½in/6cm from begin. Cont I-cord as foll:

Rows 1: K2 tog, k across—6 sts.

Rows 2–3, 5: K.

Row 4: K2 tog, k across—5 sts.

Row 6: K2 tog, k across. Cut yarn, leaving a long tail. Thread tail through rem 4 sts, gather tightly and fasten off, weave in ends.

FINISHING AND ASSEMBLY

Weave in all ends, leaving tail from CO for sewing. Following embroidery stitch guide, embroider eyes, nose, and mouth on face. With A, sew head piece tog at center back using mattress stitch. Lightly stuff head, body, and front legs. Whipstitch ears to sides of head. Use duplicate stitch to attach head to opening at top of body. Stuff bottoms of back legs and carefully attach hip to side of body with leg opening wrapping slightly to the front. Lightly stuff hip before completing seam. Sew tail in place.

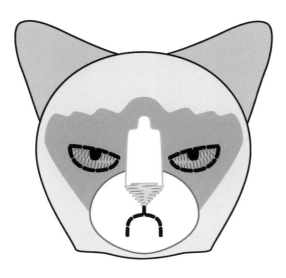

EMBROIDERY STITCH GUIDE

- Back Stitch—doubled black embroidery floss (12 ply)
- Satin Stitch—in yarn color D, split in half (2 ply)
- Satin Stitch—doubled pink embroidery floss (12 ply)

PAIN IN MY NECK CAT SCARF

DESIGNED BY CAROL HOARE

SKILL LEVEL
Intermediate

FINISHED MEASUREMENTS 5½in/14cm x 66in/167.5cm (not including legs or tail)

MATERIALS

- Berroco Ultra® Alpaca 3½oz/100g, 215yd/198m (50% alpaca, 50% wool)—two skeins #62300 Goose Bay (A), one skein each #6211 Duncan (B), #6201 Winter White (C)
- Size US 10 (6mm) needles
- One set double-pointed needles size US 10 (6.0mm) OR SIZE TO OBTAIN GAUGE
- Stitch holders
- Tapestry needle

GAUGE

13 sts and 24 rows = 4in/10cm in Garter st. TAKE TIME TO CHECK GAUGE.

Note: Yarn is held double throughout.

STITCH GUIDE

Short Row Wrap and Turn (w&t)

On RS row, slip next stitch purlwise wyib. Bring yarn forward, then slip the stitch back onto left needle. Return yarn to back. One stitch is wrapped. Turn the work. Use the same method on WS row, bringing the yarn back and then forward.

BODY

With A, CO 26 sts, using a Provisional Cast On.

Row 1 (RS): K1, m1, k to last 3 sts, skp k1.

Row 2: K.

Repeat Rows 1–2 in foll stripe pattern:

20 rows with 2 strands A.

6 rows with 1 strand each of A and B held tog.

6 rows with 1 strand each of A and C held tog.

6 rows with 1 strand each of A and B held tog.
Repeat stripe pattern 5 times.
Next Row (RS): With A, BO 2, k to last 3 sts, skp, k1.
Next Row (WS): K.
Rep last 2 rows until 5 sts remain. BO 2, k2tog, k1—2 sts.

HEAD

Turn, k2, pick up and knit 13 sts along end of scarf—15 sts.
Row 1 (RS): K1, m1, k1, m1, k11, m1, k1, m1, k1—19 sts.
Rows 2, 4, 6, 8, 10, 12: K.
Row 3: K1, m1, k1, m1, k15, m1, k1, m1, k1—23 sts.
Row 5: K1, m1, k1, m1, k19, m1, k1, m1, k1—27 sts.
Row 7: K3, m1, k1, m1, k19, m1, k1, m1, k3—31 sts.

EARS

Row 9: K10, w&t, k5, turn, k21, w&t, k5, turn, k10.
Row 11: K8, m1, k2, m1, k10, m1, k2, m1, k8—35 sts.
Row 13: With B, k5, kfb 8 times, k9, kfb 8 times, k5—51 sts.
Row 14: K13, kfb, k23, kfb, k13—53 sts.
Row 15: K5, BO 15, k 5 more sts (there will be 6 sts to the left of the BO sts), m1, k1, m1, k6, BO 15, k to end—25 sts.
Row 16: K4, k2togtbl, k13, k2togtbl, k4—23 sts.
Row 17: K to last 4 sts. Sl 4 sts onto dpn and fold to WS of work, turn.
Row 18: [K1, k1 from dpn] 4 times, k to last 8 sts, sl last 4 sts onto dpn and fold to WS of work, [k1 from dpn, k1] 4 times, pick up 1 st from previous row and 1 st from back of BO edge of ear.
Row 19: K across, pick up 1 st from BO edge of ear and 1 from prev row—27 sts.
Rows 20, 23, 24, 26: K.
Row 21: K1, skp 2 times, k17, k2tog 2 times, k1—23 sts.
Row 22: K1, skp 2 times, k13, k2tog 2 times, k1—19 sts.

NICE SCARF,
BUT NOT AS
CUTE AS I AM.

EYES

Row 25: K3, p5, k3, p5, k3.

Row 27: With C, k7, w&t, k3, w&t, k11, w&t, k3, turn, k7.

Row 28: K6, turn, k2, w&t, k11, w&t, k2, turn, k6.

Row 29: K1, skp 2 times, p2, k5, p2, k2tog 2 times, k1—15 sts.

Rows 30, 32–34. 36: K.

Row 31: K1, skp 2 times, k5, k2tog 2 times, k1—11 sts.

Row 35: K1, skp 2 times, k1, k2tog 2 times, k1—7 sts.

Row 37: K1, skp, k1, k2tog, k—5 sts.

SNOUT

Row 38: With A, K.

Row 39: P2tog, k1, p2tog, fasten off drawing tail through rem sts.

FRONT LEGS (make 2)

Hold scarf WS facing with head down. With C, pick up and knit 7 sts at edge (near base of ear) in pick-up row for head—7 sts.

K 22 rows with C, 8 rows with B.

PAW

Rows 1, 3, 6, 7: With C, K.

Row 2: K1, kfb, k3, kfb, k1—9 sts.

Row 4: K7, w&t, k5, w&t, k to end.

Row 5: K5, w&t, k3, w&t, k to end.

Row 8: K1, skp, k3, k2tog, k1—7 sts.

Row 9: K1, skp, k1, k2tog, k1—5 sts.

Row 10: BO, fasten off.

HIND END

With A, pick up 25 sts of provisional cast on.

Next Row (RS): BO 2, k to last 3 sts, skp, k1.

Next Row (WS): K.

Rep last 2 rows until 4 sts remain. BO 2, k2tog, turn, BO 2, fasten off.

Row 1: Pick up and knit 16 sts along end of scarf.

Rows 2–5, 7: K.

Row 6: K1, m1, k1, m1, k12, m1, k1, m1, k1—20 sts.

Row 8: K1, m1, k1, m1, k16, m1, k1, m1, k1—24 sts.

Row 9: K10 and slip onto holder, k4, slip last 10 sts onto holder.

TAIL

Row 10: Working on center 4 sts, pick up and knit 1 st on each end of row—6 sts.

Work in St st, slipping first st on each row, work 10 rows with C, and 40 rows with B.

Using only one strand of yarn, work 12 rows, BO, fasten off.

LEFT LEG

Row 1: Sl sts from holder to needle. With RS facing, join C and k—10 sts.
Row 2: K8, w&t, k6, w&t, k to end.
Row 3 & all odd rows: K.
Row 4: K7, w&t, k6, w&t, k to end.
Row 6: K8, w&t, k6, w&t, k to end.
Row 8: K1, skp, k1, k2tog, k1, skp, k1—7 sts.
K 22 rows with C, 8 rows with B.
Work paw as for front leg.

RIGHT LEG

Row 1: Sl sts from holder to needle. With RS facing, join C and k—10 sts.
Rows 2, 4, 6: K.
Row 3: K8, w&t, k6, w&t, k to end.
Row 5: K7, w&t, k6, w&t, k to end.
Row 7: K8, w&t, k6, w&t, k to end.
Row 8: K1, skp, k1, k2tog, k1, skp, k1—7sts.
Knit 22 rows with C, 8 rows with B.
Work paw as for front leg.

FINISHING

With B, embroider eyes, nose, and mouth as illustrated. Weave in ends.

DO NOT DISTURB CAT BED
DESIGNED BY LISA BUCCELLATO

The Pillow Cover is worked flat, folded and seamed for pillow form. The Cat Bed is worked in the round as well as back and forth in rows. When finished, sections of St st will form 4 rings, and 3 sections of Rev st st will form gussets. The St st rings are seamed from the inside of bed, and filled with polyester fiber. The gussets keep the tubes stacked in place. There are 3 windows: one on Ring 2 near the tail tip, and two on Ring 3. These are formed by working sections of St st back and forth in rows, the first st of every row is slipped. During finishing, a strand of yarn is threaded through the slipped sts, then tightened to close the filled tubes.

SKILL LEVEL

Intermediate

FINISHED MEASUREMENTS

Pillow diameter 14in/35.5cm; Bed interior diameter 15in/38cm, 8in/20cm tall

MATERIALS

- Lion Brand® Vanna's Choice® 3½oz/110g,170yds/156m (100% acrylic)—4 skeins #125 Taupe (A); 3 skeins #127 Espresso (B)

- Size US 9 (5.5mm) circular needles, one 36in/91.5cm long, and two circular needles, 24in/61cm long OR SIZE TO OBTAIN GAUGE

- One pair size US 9 (5.5mm) straight needles

- One size H-8/5.0mm crochet hook

- Stitch markers, stitch holder, and tapestry needle

- 16oz/454g polyester stuffing

- One 14in/35.5cm circular pillow form

- Eight ¾in/2cm buttons

- Small fabric bag of catnip, small bell, small blue bow (optional)

GAUGE

20 sts and 25 rows = 4in/10cm in St st. TAKE TIME TO CHECK GAUGE.

STITCH GUIDE

Sl 1 Slip 1 st with yarn held to WS.
Gusset (worked in rows over any number of sts)
Rows 1, 3, 5, 7 (RS): Sl 1, purl to end.
Rows 2, 4, 6, 8: Sl 1, knit to end.
Work Rows 1–8 once for Gusset.

PILLOW COVER

Bottom

With B, CO 30 sts.

Rows 1–5: K.

Row 6 (RS) (inc): K5, M1, k to last 5 sts, M1, k5—32 sts.

Row 7: K5, p to last 5 sts, k5.

Rows 8–35: Rep row 6–7—60 sts.

Row 36 K.

Row 37 K5, p to last 5 sts, k5.

Rows 38–65: Rep row 36–37, or until piece measures 10in/25.5cm from beg.

Row 66 (dec): K4, ssk, k to last 6 sts, k2tog, k4—58 sts.

Row 67: K5, p to last 5 sts, k5.

Rows 68–95: Rep row 66–67—30 sts.

Rows 96–100: K.

Top

Rows 101–173: Rep row 1–73—46 sts.

Row 174 (Buttonholes): K2, yo, k2tog, k1, ssk, knit to last 6 sts, k2tog, k1, yo, k2tog, k1—44 sts.

Row 175: K5, p to last 5 sts, k5.

Row 176 (dec): K4, ssk, k to last 6 sts, k2tog, k4—42 sts.

Rows 177–189: Rep row 175–176 6 times—30 sts.

Row 190: K5, purl to last 5 sts, k5.

Rows 191–193: K.

Row 194 (WS) (Buttonholes): K2, yo, k2tog, knit to last 3 sts, yo, k2tog, k1.

Rows 195–196: K. BO knitwise on WS.

FINISHING

Fold pillow cover in half across garter ridge. Sew buttons to WS of bottom, opposite buttonholes. Sew side edges together beginning at the fold, work to the end of the straight side edges leaving the button/buttonhole edges open for pillow insertion. Insert pillow form, button the cover closed.

EARS

With straight needles, CO 25 sts.

Row 1: (RS) Sl 1, k11, pm, sl 1, k to end.

Rows 2 and all WS rows: Sl 1, purl to end.

Rows 3, 7, 11: Sl 1, k to 2 sts before marker, sl 1, k2tog, k to end—23 sts.

Rows 5, 9, 13: Sl 1, k to marker, sl 1, k11.

Rows 15–25: RS rows only Rep row 3—7 sts.

Row 27: Sl 1, skp, sl 1, k2tog, k1—5 sts.

Row 29: Sl 1, s2pk, k1—3 sts.

Row 30: (WS) P3tog. Fasten off, cut yarn, leaving a tail for seaming.

FINISHING

With WS tog, fold in half along the center slipped st and sew the side edges together. Fill with a little fiber, sew cast-on edge closed.

BED

With B and longest circular needle, CO 188 sts. Join to work in the round, being careful not to twist sts, place marker for beg of rnd.

Knit 4 rnds.

Ring 1—Tail

Next rnd (inc): [K4, M1] 47 times—235 sts.

Knit 18 rnds.

Divide for tail tip

Slip last 8 sts on holder for tail tip and hold to front of work.

Next rnd: K227, CO 8 sts—235 sts. Pm on the 4th st for loop placement later. Leave beg of rnd marker in place.

Next rnd: (dec) [K3, k2tog] 47 times—188 sts.

Knit 3 rnds. Set aside while you work tail tip.

TAIL TIP

Slip 8 tail sts to straight needles, join B.

Next row (RS): K8, CO 9 sts—17 sts.

Purl next row and all even-numbered (WS) rows.

Row 1 (RS): K17.

Row 3 (dec): K7, s2pk, k7—15 sts.

Rows 5, 7, 11 and 13: K7, pm, sl 1, k7.

Rows 15–23 (dec) RS rows only: K2tog, k to marker, sl 1, k to last 2 sts, ssk—5 sts.

Row 25: K2tog, sl 1, ssk—3 sts.

Row 26 (WS): P3tog. Fasten off.

Fold tail along slipped st with WS tog, seam along curved side edges. Fill tail tip with fiber. Sew CO edge of tail to marked CO edge of St st section, leaving a small opening at marker for catnip bag insertion.

BUTTON LOOP

With crochet hook, join B to marked st. Chain 8, join with slip st to first chain to form button loop. Fasten off. Sew a button to tail tip above the opening, opposite button loop. Return to work Ring 1.

Divide for Window

Next row (RS): With B, BO 8 sts for tail window, change to A, cut B, p to end—180 sts. Remove beg of rnd marker, turn to work in rows.

Next row (WS): Sl 1, k179.

Work Rows 3–8 of Gusset over 180 sts.

Ring 2 with Tail Window

Next row (RS): Sl 1, k179.

Slip first st of every row and work 3 rows St st.

Next row (inc): Sl 1, k3, M1, [k4, M1] 44 times—225 sts.

Next row (WS): Sl 1, p224.

Slip first st of every row and work 18 rows St st.

Next rnd (dec): Sl 1, k2, k2tog, [k3, k2tog] 44 times—180 sts.

Slip first st of every row and work 3 rows St st.

Ring 3 with Side and Eye Windows

Divide for windows

Note: Work will be divided into 3 sections: A, B, and C. Section B is worked separately in rows. Sections A and C are worked in rows, separately at first and then joined. When windows are complete, all sections will be joined to work in the round.

Set-up row (RS): Sl 1, p49 for Section A, leave needle and yarn to be worked later; with shorter circular needle and second ball of A, BO 8 sts for side window, p until there are 64 sts on the RH needle after the BO for Section B. Turn to work Section B in rows.

Section B

Work Rows 2–8 of Gusset over 64 sts.

Next row (RS): Sl 1, k63.

Slip first st of every row and work 3 rows St st.

Inc row (RS): [K4, M1] 15 times, k3, M1, k1—80 sts.

Next row (WS): Sl 1, p79.

Slip first st of every row and work 18 rows St st.

Dec row (RS): [K3, k2tog] 16 times—64 sts.

Slip first st of every row and work 3 rows St st.

Work Rows 1–8 of Gusset. Set aside, cut yarn.

Section C

Next row (RS): With second shorter circular needle and new strand of A, return to remaining unworked sts and BO 8 sts for eye window, p until there are 50 sts on RH needle for Section C. Turn to work Section C in rows.

Work Rows 2–8 of Gusset over 50 sts, do not cut yarn.

Section A

Rejoin A to Section A, ready for a WS row. Work rows 2–8 of Gusset over 50 sts. Cut A.

Join Sections A and C

Next row (RS): With A, sl 1, k49 across Section C, CO 8 sts, k50 across Section A—108 sts.

Next row: Sl 1, p107.

Slip first st of every row and continue in St st for 3 more rows.

Inc row (RS): Sl 1, [k4, M1] 26 times, k3–134 sts.

Slip first st of every row and continue in St st for 19 more rows.

Dec row (RS): Sl 1, [k3, k2tog] 26 times, k3—108 sts.

Slip first st of every row and work 3 rows St st.

Work Rows 1–8 of Gusset.

Ring 4—Join all sections

Next rnd: Work all sts onto longest circular needle, pm for new beginning of rnd, k108, CO 8, k64, CO 8—188 sts. Join to work in the rnd.

Knit 3 rnds.

Inc rnd: [K4, M1] 47 times—235 sts.

Knit 19 rnds.

Dec rnd: [K3, k2tog] 47 times—188 sts.

Knit 3 rnds. BO.

FINISHING

Sew and Fill Rings: Working on Rings 2 and 3, with tapestry needle pull a 10in/25.5cm length of A through each line of slipped sts at end of each St st section.

From the inside of bed, fold Ring 4 with bound off edge meeting Row 8 of adjacent gusset to form a tube. Sew edges tog, stuffing as you go. Do not over stuff, the fiber will show through the knitting.

Fold Ring 1 with CO edge meeting Row 1 of adjacent gusset and BO edge of window. Sew edges tog and stuff.

Fold Ring 2 with Row 8 of previous gusset meeting Row 1 of next gusset, match BO and CO edges of window openings. Sew and fill. Pull the lengths of yarn to close the row ends, fasten off and weave in. Work Ring 3 in same manner.

Attach Ears: Using photo on page 48 as a guide, position ears on either side of the eye window, and sew the CO edge of ear to the inside of the top ring along the seam. Baste front of ear to the inside of the ring for extra support.

If desired, sew small bell to tail tip, place catnip bag in tail opening, and sew small blue bow in eye window.

GRUMPY CAT PULLOVERS FOR THE WHOLE FAMILY

DESIGNED BY MARGEAU SOBOTI

SHOWN IN WOMEN'S SMALL AND CHILDREN'S SIZE 6 (See page 57.)

SKILL LEVEL

Experienced

SIZES

Women's Small (Medium, Large); Men's (Small, Medium, Large); Children's size (6, 8, 10).

FINISHED MEASUREMENTS

Bust/chest 36 (40, 44) (38, 42, 46) (28, 30, 32)in/91.5 (101.5, 112) (96.5, 106.5, 117) (71, 76, 81.5)cm

Length 22¼ (23½, 24½) (23½, 24½, 25½) (16, 17, 18)in/56.5 (59.5, 62) (59.5, 62, 64.5) (40.5, 43, 45.5)cm

Upper arm 12 (13, 14) (13½, 14, 15) (9, 9½, 10)in/30.5 (33, 35.5) (34.5, 35.5, 38) (23, 24, 25.5)cm

MATERIALS

FOR WOMEN'S AND MEN'S SIZES

• Lion Brand® Collection® Baby Alpaca 1¾oz/50g, 146yd/133m (100% Baby Alpaca): 6 (7, 8) (7, 8, 9) one ball each: #098 Natural (MC), 1 ball each: #124 Tan (A), #125 Fawn Heather (B), #126 Auburn (C), #153 Black (D)

FOR CHILDREN'S SIZES

• Berroco® Comfort® DK 1¾oz/50g, 178yd/165m (50% Nylon, 50% Acrylic): 3 (4, 5) ball in #2703 Barley (MC), #2720 Hummus (A), #2771 Driftwood Heather (B), #2727 Spanish Brown (C), #2734 Liquorice (D)

• One pair size US 4 (3.5mm) needles OR SIZE TO OBTAIN GAUGE

• Size 3 circular needle, 16in/40.5cm long

• Stitch markers, tapestry needle, and bobbins (optional)

GAUGE

23 sts and 31 rows = 4in/10cm in St st on larger needles. TAKE TIME TO CHECK GAUGE.

STITCH GUIDE

K1, P1 Rib (odd number of sts). **Row 1 (RS):** K1, [p1, k1] across.

Row 2 (WS): P1, [k1, p1] across. Rep Rows 1 and 2 for k1, p1 rib.

NOTES

1. When using the long tail CO, begin with a WS row. The long tail CO makes the CO plus one row.

2. Use intarsia method for color work. Twist yarn on back of work when changing colors. Do NOT carry yarn across. Use bobbins if desired.

CAT CHART

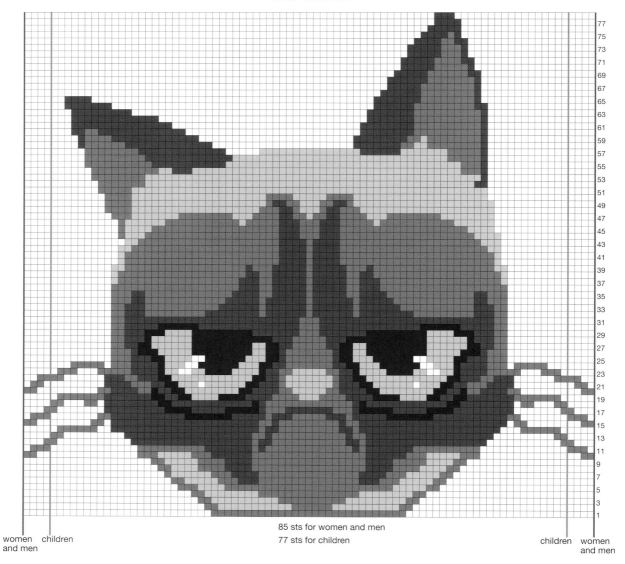

77
75
73
71
69
67
65
63
61
59
57
55
53
51
49
47
45
43
41
39
37
35
33
31
29
27
25
23
21
19
17
15
13
11
9
7
5
3
1

women and men   children

85 sts for women and men
77 sts for children

children   women and men

COLOR KEY

☐ Natural, Barley (MC)

☐ Tan, Hummus (A)

▨ Fawn Heather, Driftwood Heather (B)

▨ Auburn, Spanish Brown (C)

■ Black, Liquorice (D)

BACK

With MC, CO 103 (115, 127) (109, 121, 133) (81, 87, 93) sts. Work in k1, p1 rib until piece measures 1½ (1½) (1)in/4 (4) (2.5)cm from beg, ending with WS row. Cont in St st (k on RS, p on WS) until piece measures 12½ (13, 13½) (13, 13½, 14) (10½, 11, 11½)in/32 (33, 34.5) (33, 34.5, 35.5) (26.5, 28, 29)cm from beg, ending with WS row.

Armhole shaping

BO 6 (9, 12) (4, 8, 11) (5, 5, 6) sts at beg of next 2 rows.

Next row (dec): K2, ssk, k to last 4 sts, k2tog, k2—2 sts dec'd.

Rep dec row every other row 26 (29, 30) (29, 31, 33) (16, 18, 20) times—37 (37, 41) (41, 41, 43) (37, 39, 39) sts. BO.

FRONT

Note: Read through entire pattern before continuing. Place 2 markers, one on either side of center 85 (85) (77) sts.

For women's and men's sizes only

Work as for Back until piece measures 3½ (4, 4½) (4, 4½, 5)in/9 (10, 11.5) (10, 11.5, 12.5)cm from beg, ending with WS row.

For children's sizes only

Work as for Back until 6 (8, 8) rows have been worked in St st, ending with WS row.

Beg cat chart and neck shaping

Note: Read through entire pattern before continuing.

Next row (RS): K9 (15, 21) (12, 18, 24) (2, 5, 8), slip marker (sm), work 85 (85) (77) sts of Chart Row 1, sm, k9 (15, 21) (12, 18, 24) (2, 5, 8).

Next row (WS): P9 (15, 21) (12, 18, 24) (2, 5, 8), sm, work 85 (85) (77) sts of Chart Row 2, sm, p9 (15, 21) (12, 18, 24) (2, 5, 8).

Cont to work chart as established until piece measures 12½ (13, 13½) (13, 13½, 14) (10½, 11, 11½)in/32 (33, 34.5) (33, 34.5, 35.5) (26.5, 28, 29)cm from beg, ending with WS row.

AT SAME TIME:

Armhole shaping

For women's and men's sizes only

Cont chart and shape armholes as for Back, working dec row 21 (24, 26) (25, 27, 29) times only.

For children's sizes only

Cont cat chart and shape armholes as for Back.

NECK SHAPING

For all sizes

When there are 63 (69, 75) (73, 77, 83) (49, 51, 51) sts on needles, place second set of markers on either side of center 19 (19, 21) (21, 21, 23) (15, 17, 17) sts for neck shaping.

Next row (RS): Continuing armhole shaping, work in pat to first center neck shaping marker, join 2nd ball of yarn and BO center 19 (19, 21) (21, 21, 23) (15, 17, 17) sts, work in pat to end.

For women's and men's sizes only

Working both sides at the same time, BO from each neck edge 5 sts once, 4 sts once, 3 sts once, 2 sts once, dec 1 st. Continue armhole shaping if needed. Fasten off.

For children's sizes only

Working both sides at the same time, BO from each neck edge 4 sts once, 3 sts once, 2 sts once, dec 1 st twice. Continue armhole shaping if needed. Fasten off.

RIGHT SLEEVE

CO 41 (43, 43) (43, 47, 49) (37, 39, 41) sts. Work in k1, p1 rib until piece measures 1½ (1½) (1)in/4 (4) (2.5)cm from beg, ending with WS row. Cont in St st.

Next row (inc): K1, M1, k to last st, M1, k1—2 sts inc'd.

For women's sizes (M, L) and men's sizes (S, M, L) only

Rep inc row every 6th row 0 (7, 18) (16, 9, 9) times, then

For all sizes

Rep inc row every 8th row 13 (8, 0) (0, 7, 9) (6, 7, 7) times — 69 (75, 81) (77, 81, 87) (51, 55, 57) sts.

Cont until piece measures 17½ (17½, 18) (18, 18½, 19½) (12, 13½, 15)in/44.5 (44.5, 45.5) (45.5, 47, 50) (30.5, 34.5, 38)cm from beg, ending with WS row.

Shape cap

BO 6 (9, 12) (4, 8, 11) (6, 6, 7) sts at beg of next 2 rows.

Next row (dec): K2, ssk, k to last 4 sts, k2tog, k2—2 sts dec'd.

Rep dec row every other row 2 (2, 1) (14, 9, 7) (9, 11, 9) times, then every 4th row 11 (11, 12) (5, 8, 10) (3, 3, 5) times—29 (29) (13) sts.

For women's and men's sizes only

Shape top of cap

Beg of next RS row, BO 7 sts once, 6 sts once, 5 sts once, 4 sts twice, 3 sts once.

For children's sizes only

BO.

LEFT SLEEVE

Work as for Right Sleeve.

For women's and men's sizes only

Reverse shape top of cap by working BO rows at beg of WS rows.

FINISHING

Set in raglan sleeves. Sew sides and sleeve seams.

Neck Band

With RS facing, using circular needles, and beg at back of right shoulder, pick up and knit 34 (34, 36) (36, 36, 40) (34, 34, 36) sts evenly along back of neck, 27 (27) (11) sts along top of left sleeve, 54 (54, 56) (56, 56, 58) (38, 40, 40) sts evenly along front of neck, 27 (27) (11) sts along top of right sleeve—142 (142, 146) (146, 146, 152) (94, 96, 98) sts.

Place marker, join in rnd.

Work in k1, p1 rib until neck band measures 1in/2.5cm. BO. Weave in ends. Block lightly to finished measurements.

SCHEMATIC FOR CHILD'S SWEATER

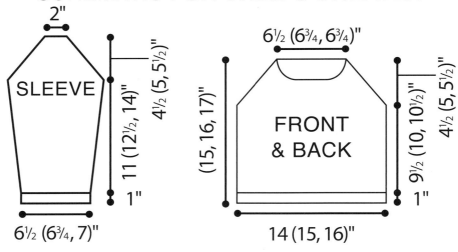

2"

SLEEVE

4½ (5, 5½)"

11 (12½, 14)"

1"

6½ (6¾, 7)"

6½ (6¾, 6¾)"

FRONT
& BACK

(15, 16, 17)"

4½ (5, 5½)"

9½ (10, 10½)"

1"

14 (15, 16)"

SCHEMATIC FOR ADULT'S SWEATER

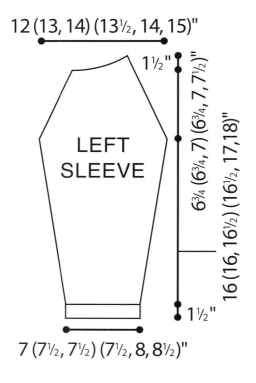

12 (13, 14) (13½, 14, 15)"

1½"

LEFT
SLEEVE

6¾ (6¾, 7) (6¾, 7, 7½)"

16 (16, 16½) (16½, 17, 18)"

1½"

7 (7½, 7½) (7½, 8, 8½)"

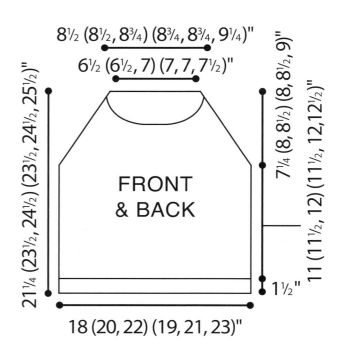

8½ (8½, 8¾) (8¾, 8¾, 9¼)"

6½ (6½, 7) (7, 7, 7½)"

21¼ (23½, 24½) (23½, 24½, 25½)"

FRONT
& BACK

7¼ (8, 8½) (8, 8½, 9)"

11 (11½, 12) (11½, 12, 12½)"

1½"

18 (20, 22) (19, 21, 23)"

WISHY-WASHY WASHCLOTH CHART

FROM PAGES 26-27

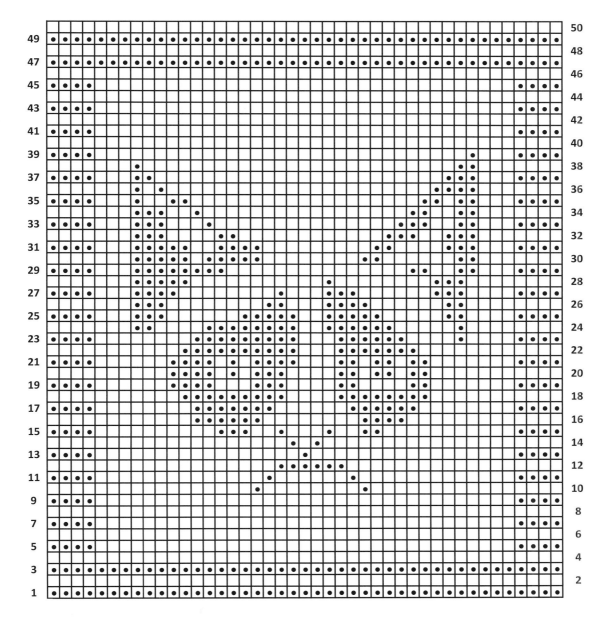

KEY

☐ Knit on RS and Purl on WS

⊡ Purl on RS and Knit on WS

ABBREVIATIONS

approx	approximately		RC	right cross
beg	begin/beginning		rem	remain/remaining
BO	bind off		rep	repeat
CC	contrasting color		Rev st st	reverse stockinette stitch
ch	chain		rnd(s)	round(s)
cm	centimeter(s)		RPC	right purl cross
cn	cable needle		RS	right side
CO	cast on		sc	single crochet
cont	continue		sc2tog	single crochet two together
dec	decrease/decreases/decreasing		skp	slip, knit, pass stitch over—one stitch decreased
dpn(s)	double-pointed needle(s)		sk2p	slip 1, knit 2 together, pass slip stitch over the knit 2 together—2 stitches decreased
foll	follow/follows/following			
g	gram			
in	inches		sl	slip
inc	increase/increases/increasing		sm	slip marker
k or K	knit		Sp2p	slip stitch as if to purl, purl two together, pass the slipped stitch over the purl two together
kwise	knitwise			
k2tog	knit 2 stitches together			
k3tog	knit 3 stitches together		ssk	slip, slip, knit these 2 stitches together—a decrease
kfb	knit in front and back—increase			
LC	left cross		ssp	slip next 2 stitches as if to knit, slip them back to the left needle and purl them together through the back loops
lp(s)	loop(s)			
LPC	left purl cross			
MC	main color			
M1	make one			
M1R	make one right		st(s)	stitch(es)
M1L	make one left		St st	stockinette stitch/stocking stitch
mm	millimeters		tog	together
oz	ounces		WS	wrong side
p or P	purl		wyib	with yarn in back
pat	pattern(s)		wyif	with yarn in front
pm	place marker		yd(s)	yard(s)
p2tog	purl 2 stitches together		yfwd	yarn forward
			yo	yarn over